About the Author

Dorothy "Dora" Dickey (nee Fenwick) was born during 1910 at Newcastle-on-Tyne in the United Kingdom. Dorothy, together with her mother and siblings, emigrated to Australia shortly after the First World War. Following a short stay in Sydney, New South Wales, the Fenwick family settled into the historic City of Maitland, (Gadigal Country) located North of Sydney, New South Wales. She spent some time as a house servant at the renowned Aberglasslyn House, located at East Maitland, where she was inspired to write verse about natural beauty. Shortly after her stay at Aberglasslyn House, she met and married Ronald Dickey and they settled into a small house in Lindsay Street, East Maitland. It was in this warm and welcoming place that she was inspired to write many poems about her love for God and family, about birth, about life and about death. A booklet of her earlier poems has existed for many years in the Maitland City Library.

Nanna's Poems
Cradle to the Grave Verse

Lord Christopher

Nanna's Poems
Cradle to the Grave Verse

Olympia Publishers
London

www.olympiapublishers.com
OLYMPIA PAPERBACK EDITION

Copyright © Lord Christopher 2023

The right of Lord Christopher to be identified as author of
this work has been asserted in accordance with sections 77 and 78 of
the Copyright, Designs and Patents Act 1988.

All Rights Reserved

No reproduction, copy or transmission of this publication
may be made without written permission.
No paragraph of this publication may be reproduced,
copied or transmitted save with the written permission of the publisher,
or in accordance with the provisions
of the Copyright Act 1956 (as amended).

Any person who commits any unauthorised act in relation to
this publication may be liable to criminal
prosecution and civil claims for damage.

A CIP catalogue record for this title is
available from the British Library.

ISBN: 978-1-80439-091-7

This is a work of fiction.
Names, characters, places and incidents originate from the writer's
imagination. Any resemblance to actual persons, living or dead, is
purely coincidental. The following poems respect the original set out by
the author, Dorothy Dickey

First Published in 2023

Olympia Publishers
Tallis House
2 Tallis Street
London
EC4Y 0AB

Printed in Great Britain

Dedication

I dedicate this book to my beloved grandmother, Dorothy Dora Dickey (nee Fenwick) and to my grandfather Ronald Dickey. Thank you so very much for your care, love and attention during my formative years. I am what I am because of your dedication to my welfare. I love you and I miss you.

Acknowledgements

Thank you so very much to my beautiful wife Anne for being so patient during the time I needed to put Nanna's poetic journey together. Thank you also to Sandy and Terry Odgers for your invaluable input during the draft preparation of "Nanna's Poems".

Preamble:

In loving memory
Author Dorothy Fenwick pictured with husband Ronald Dickey.
Thank you, Dear God, for our grandparents,
For they both were heaven sent.

Nanna's Poems is a poignant collection about *life*. The collection spins a bittersweet tale of childhood, marriage and death. For Dora, the one consistency in her life was God. Though temptation is everywhere and the world in which we live is such a harrowing one, at its heart, this collection explores the power of His love and His guidance.

I am very pleased, as one of the many Grandson's of Dora, to commend my Grandmothers poems to you.

I hope you find Dora's poems moving.

– *Lord Christopher*

Introduction

What is this life? Why are we here? Our journey starts when we fight our way down the birth canal and arrive into an alien world. Some arrive angry. Some arrive happy.

We arrive helpless. We arrive vulnerable. For the first quarter of our lives we need lots of love and protection. We also need education about how to "*live*". During this time we learn the main rules of life: how to survive and how to thrive.

We become educated. We become strong. We seek our independence and so then venture into the challenging world around us. We intend to make our own way and, in so doing, stamp our own mark on this world. Some do. Some don't.

We are gregarious. We seek alike company. We seek love. Courtship follows. Some of us marry. Some don't. We breed.

Suddenly middle age arrives. We start to reflect on what we have achieved. We think that in some instances we should have done things a little better. Some of us have regrets.

Then old age arrives. We struggle to remain healthy. We struggle to remain upright. We wish we didn't have that niggling pain. We do things at a pace far less than when we wore a younger person's clothes.

Death comes knocking. Our partner passes on and then we find ourselves alone. We sit around and can do nothing more than to wait to die.

Finally we die. Suddenly revelation: the reason why we were born in the first place.

My grandmother wrote many poems about life's journey. I hope you enjoy her verse. I also hope you are moved and also comforted, if needed, by her words.

But at night, when all the world's asleep
The questions run so deep
For such a simple man
Won't you please tell me what we've learned
I know it sounds absurd
Please tell me who I am?

Courtesy: Super-tramp 1979

Lord Christopher

God and Creation

Is My God calling?

Hark! I hear the breeze passing through tall trees
The breeze generates soft sounds from each leaf falling
My peaceful thoughts result from this breeze
To me, this is the voice of my God calling;
He also whispers to me as He doth go
Walking so softly over the many grasses
It is as if they all murmur in a co-ordinated voice so low.
"Rejoice for this is the way our Lord passes."

I see the rain splash onto my windowpane
And on my rooftop, it keeps beating
It seems to me that these things, again
Give me a sign that my God is not sleeping
His call is so clear upon a Sabbath morn
As I hear the local church bells ringing
Seems to me our faith again is reborn
And I hear the voice of His angels singing.

I look up into the morning sky
And I see a blue bird is soaring
The blue bird seems to fly so high
It seems to me it's heart is pouring
Out such love for its creation

And behold! so humble these the willow trees
Over the river they keep bending
As though they want to sneak a daily peek
Of each blessing our God is sending.

And we who know he loves us so
We should never be despairing
When this earth is prone to leave us alone.
There is always One who is caring
Day by day, come what may
Be it good or evil falling
We will always hear through our sadness or fear
The voice of our God calling.

An Ageless Dawning

Hello, morning light! You make my day so bright!
You summon me from my slumber to arise
Such another beautiful morn… a new day born
Brings much pleasure to my sleepy eyes.

So much magic abounding in the cool morning air
So very fresh and clean it seems
It intrudes into my sleepy mind
And calls me out of my unworldly dreams.

Oh, morning fair! Oh, morning light!
You dispel my darkness suffered through last night
In slumber land I did hear you call, oh my Lord
Heralding that a brand new day is about to be born.

I look and see glistening raindrops upon every rose
Where the sun flits its magic repose
Each rose shines like jewels upon the grass
And so mark my worldly footprints as I pass.

I hear the birds twittering far off in the trees
And I then thank my God for such as these
They too find magic in each brand new morn;
They serenade each new day born.

Was it only yesterday we lost our dream?
Was hope gone… in this modern world it would seem
But there is hope in every new morn!
A regeneration in each new beautiful and colourful dawn.

Mustard Seed

Life's brutality has caused me to doubt my dedication
To my Lord whom I now seem to have forsaken.

I so longed for a faith that always would be big and strong
So I could move mountains… so I could part the sea
I strived so very hard with my faith… but something was very wrong.

All I could see was a tiny mustard seed of faith buried inside of me.

So, I asked myself, "How does one's faith grow?
Is it like a garden full of flowers?"
Then I heard a voice inside me say, "Hello!"
Only through thoughtful, prayerful hours
Delivering what cannot be seen
A world beyond my touch
A prince who died to set us all free
The building blocks of faith are such.

To know that my God walked along my way
And though my faith is sometimes dim
My faith is able to burst forth from my mustard seed
By thoughtful and loving fellowship with Him.

Through dedicated prayer I beheld my mustard seed
I saw it started to grow into a tiny tree
It had sprung forth from my doubtful heart;
Its branches commenced to shelter me
My faith became so strong I know I can move
Those far off mountains into the sea.

Now if you have a tiny mustard seed
There planted somewhere in your heart
And you long to grow a sturdy tree
But your seed just won't get a start
Don't give up hope and then let it die
Because of your worldly despair
Your seed needs a lot of nourishing
So delve into constant meaningful prayer
Keep God within and soon you will find
A gigantic faithful tree grows within!

There is no boundary to our God's love;
His love seems to be far wider than the sea;
His love permeates throughout all our world
There is no escape... His love will find both you and me.

Way of the Cross

There is just one way that we all will go
To dwell with our God in the morning
We will travel the way that is worn so
And all other ways we must be scorning.

The way is a flower strewn path that we must go;
Our transition will be so full of song and dancing
Beware, selfishness leads you to a darker place
So don't leave your life's choice to chancing.

The way of the cross is often hard
And along the way, many a storm may find us
But by keeping your eyes on the hillside there
And so that holy cross will find us
If we spend our life in love and prayer
We will meet Jesus in the morning
And oh, such joy when we meet him there
Greetings just as a new day is dawning.

The road is not broad… it is a shining way
Enhanced by the sound of the Angel's chorus
We cannot slip if we walk the way of the cross
So keep the old rugged cross before us
We may fight jungle or briar patch
Where the thorns will rip and tear at us;

We may hear wild beasts as they growl and roar
Around the route to try and scare us.

God help us all to walk the way of the cross
For it leads to forgiving light in the dawning
And behold the star of David glowing there
So bright and holy in the new morning
Through jungle wild… or the shining way
I will keep to the set path before me;
I will walk in the shadow of the cross He bore
And so I will meet Jesus in the morning.

Birth and Children

First Christmas

O' hear the song heaven's angels sing
And this is what they say:
To Mary, there in Bethlehem
Behold a son is born this day
His name is Jesus… a beautiful babe
Inside a modest cattle shed
And lo! the star of hope divine
Is beaming clearly overhead.

God has kept the long-term promise
He made many many years ago
Because of the wall of darkness, it has crept
All over His wonderful creation below;
Gun and knife… selfishness, hate and strife
Has swept across our land –
For what our God was really like
Lost souls refused to understand.

Humble child, so meek and so mild
With cattle he did lay
Because of him who comes to free us
We celebrate this our Christmas day
So Mary please rest… by God you are so blessed

With your holy boy child
For He has come to save this world
And drive all of our sinfulness away.

A Child's Secret Place

There is a secret garden kept in a child's heart
Where lovely thoughts do nurture and grow;
When they want to commune with God
It is to their secret place they do go.

When heavy burdens do bear them down
To their secret place they do flee
And find sweet comfort for their soul
So then in flows peace and tranquillity.

There are huge trees storing love, faith and hope;
Each one stands stately, tall and serene
And all their leaves are sprinkled all over with
Their every fragrant dream.

Bright crystal waters do gently flow
From Heaven through this place they go
And wicked shadows never dare
To intrude into this secret place
Because the child sits and talk to Jesus there.

Energy of Children

How would life be without our little kids?
For love and company –
More peaceful without them?
Yes, it may be so
And certainly much less noise
Without the constant noise from those little girls and boys.

They have so much "go" in each of them
And when each day is done
Our "go" has almost vanished
Whilst theirs keeps going on!

Those little kids always keep us poor
But we enjoy our spending
The spending is our joy for sure
They may give us headaches
And keep us on our toes
But we are so very proud of all our kids
It is for sure… everyone knows!
We boast so very much about them
Till everyone is so bored
But such amusing incidents
In our minds forever stored.

Kids, kids, they drive us off our lids!

There are times when we want to sell them
If we could get any bids... that is!
For all the things they should not do
You cannot get them to do it
It's 'Gary, stop your fighting'
And 'Terry, go wash your face!'
No matter how much we yell at them
They put you in your place.

They trek their muddy footprints
Across a freshly cleaned floor
And you will find their little fingerprints
On every pantry door
When at last they become weary
And into bed they creep
We thank their guardian angels
To guide them off to sleep!

Overactive Son

I have an overactive son;
He's always on the go
"Hey, Mum, can I do this for fun?"
Oh, my tension headaches hurt me so.

My son takes the fruit off our trees
And sells them around the block
And when he fights with other boys
Our whole suburb seems to rock.

He is such a little dynamo
Who never admits to defeat;
He will bash into the bigger boys
'Till he knocks them off their feet.

He plays cricket… he is so very keen
So much so he takes his bat to bed
And perhaps he wants it blessed by God too
Within the prayers he has just said.

He likes to wash our breakfast things
But he nearly floods us out
He is quick with what he does
Oh, dear… there is water all about!

Whenever his friends do not want to play
He bribes them with my food;
My biscuits and the fruit go down
A little bit quicker than they should.

Oh, we love our little dynamo
But we long for his engine to stall
That is when he longs for bed so
It is then to bed we all do crawl.

Little Kids!

Finally, when they are fast asleep
It is then that we start to think
Oh, how empty our lives would be
If there were no little kids
To drain all our energy.

Kids! kids! we need them… always did!
Each kid reminds us of our innocence
That from us now may be hid
Kids are not saints… they are not meant to be;
But inside each little child
There is a sweetness that you and me have lost, you see
Kids are oh so innocent… not like you nor me.

And then there is something to remember:
When we are flat… on the skids
Long long ago there was a time
When we adults were those kids
We were just as naughty back then
And I'm sure we drove our parents mad;
It is a fact we oft forget
Because we are now Mum's and Dad's.

Bedtime Stories

Remember when you were so very small
And time for your sleep was not far away?
Off to bed, you and your teddy would crawl
Leaving behind all your thoughts of the day.

As you would lay there in your comfy bed
With your eyes wide open and so bright
Ready to receive your bedtime story so far unread
I would turn down your light and see you excite!

How you loved each story that would unfold
And I loved the telling of each one too
It made me feel so happy to see how you glowed
Dear to my heart my audience of one… it was you!

When soon your eyes grew droopy for sleep
Then I would rise and tip toe out your door
Sometimes though the road to sleep seemed long
And you would beg me please to tell some more.

Ah, how the years have flown by since then
And how the world has turned its face around
For no one tells the bedtime stories now
Since the thrill of the smart phone world was found.

Where Is Our Red Riding Hood?

She wore a red coat with a little red snood
So we all called her little Red-Riding-Hood
With her shining curls, and her eyes so blue
She could charm the socks right off you
She was so loving and oh so very good
Our darling little Red-Riding-Hood.

Each morning she would creep into our bed
For she loved to "cuddle up", that is what she said
She would hold our hands wherever we went
And we thanked the Lord for this child He sent
Each year, as she grew, we bought her anew
A little red coat, and matching red shoes too.

It seemed so fitting, for we thought she would
Forever be our little Red-Riding-Hood
But the years move fast, soon childhood doth pass
Like the budding red rose and the green green grass
Then the changes come as I guessed they would
And we lost the attention of our Red-Riding-Hood.

For those few short years we were always three
So very proud of her dad and me
But one day we looked, and a woman stood
In place of our little Red-Riding-Hood.

A woman who had no need of our care
And now she has gone, to some place, somewhere.

Now her coat is discarded for grown up things
So many heartaches for us this brings
We can never reach where our little child has gone
We can but pray for our little lost one;
But we will never forget – what parents could?
The love for and of our little red Red-Riding-Hood.

Love and Marriage

What Is "Love?"

So what is love?
How can it be defined?
Is it a gift from God above?
Or is it just a figment of our mind?

Our common senses are so overwhelmed
By an unbridled power so undefined –
I can tell you that I felt this when first I was held
In the arms of my first lover, so entwined!

My heart leaped from out of my breast
My breathing was so very fast
Love so overpowering me as he so pressed
I had found my first love at last.

Family scolded both of us
They say we both were far too young
They made such an unholy fuss
But all we could feel was that love had sprung.

We separated for just a little while
But human bondage does prevail
One day he caught my eye with his beautiful smile

And in that *Ship of Love* we then did finally sail.

I can now tell you that love is a yearning, a wanting
To be always close to whom you cannot do without
And I have found myself often fawning
For my true love, there is, each day, no doubt.

We have been together now for many decades
And I still turn to look for that beautiful smile
That wonderful expression that doth so invade
My senses because it says, "*Hey kid, stay with me for a while!*"

Young Love

You both are "*too young to wed!*"
Just puppy love as yet!
That is all they said,
"*Wedding vows you will regret!*"

"*It's just puppy love!*" again they cried,
"*New love, that given three months, will die!*"

"*Could never stand the human trials
Of the adult years ahead!*"

"*So young you cannot live together
And then bear the strains of life!*"
They cut our pleas to pieces
With sharp words that cut just like a knife.

So I cried, "*Farewell, my lover.*"

"*They are driving us apart.*"
"*Oh, if they only knew it.*"

"*I will be left with only half a heart.*"
I think they all have forgotten this
That such true love can endure
For our kind of pure loving

There really is no medical cure.

"*So please wait for me, my own true love.*"
"*Just a few more years ahead.*"
"*Then they cannot crush our puppy love!*"

"*That day when we two will be wed!*"

True Love

True love? Is there such a thing?
Does true love only appear during Spring?
We, you and me, have been so long together
For what seems to be timeless… forever
We started off so very very young;
We found delight in each other's fun
As we aged, we drew closer together
Just like those birds of a common feather
We faced each other over so many battles
But then we realised we didn't need those hassles
At times… when one of us was down
The other would act like a silly clown
The other would laugh…back together again
You are so much my very true friend;
There were demons coming at us many times
But you and me, we had better designs
We protectively clung to each other
So those demons we then did smother
For all of our experiences we discovered a love so true
Because we stuck together with a loving glue
But old man time has finally jumped us.
It was so stressful to witness your illness… then you did pass
After you had gone, I stumbled across your old shoe box
under our bed, My true love! it contained everything that I
had said

All my written words to you, including birthday cards
For us, now death will have no dominion
Because you, my love… are one in a million.

Battlefield

Marriage sometimes can be a battlefield
Nerves are sometimes on high alert
To meet the barrage of harsh words
That sometimes set each one of us apart.

It is then that loves' flower doth close up
Maybe for just a little while
But each bout on the lovers' battlefield
Can cause love to be defiled.

If only each half of the loving whole could be wise
And then let each express itself
Otherwise there will be less marriages
Each half of the whole keeping to itself.

Neither half is the perfect half
For true love will always absolve
Selfishness will starve the love of the whole
And so stifle and then control.

My House

Beloved house you have so sheltered me
For so many years upon this earth
But as the time arrives, I will be leaving you
To find myself a glorious rebirth.

Sweet memories of our love so true
You hold within your ageing breast
Sorrow has also walked your floors
But all of your floors the Lord has blessed.

Beloved house God gave you to me
In answer to my fervent prayer
For who will occupy when I'm gone
In every room I'll leave a prayer.

You are the only colourful house
That we both could ever call our own;
Children's voices did fill your rooms
And now there is just my voice alone.

Beloved house in you a spirit dwells
That in your heart will ever stay
While I still dwell within your walls
And also then when I'm gone one day.

Snow White and Tinted Top

You and me are "tinted top" and "snow white"
We have made such a happy pair;
You so unashamedly let nature take its course
But I would always dye my hair
I felt a need to look always so very nice
But all you could do was to protest and stare.

One day, in May, I stopped my colouring
So nature caused my hair to go oh so grey
The neighbourhood then said he had never been
The same man since that colourless day.

Although it cost you plenty
To keep me, your old, tinted top
When we both became *Snow White*
You just could not stand that shock.

So you begged me, "*Hey, old, tinted top.*"
"*Give your coloured hair another go!*"
You wanted me to put the colour back in
Because you, my love, could not stand the snow!

So Deep the Snow

When the snow doth lay so deep
So our passion does go to sleep
We will still be friends, so please, my love, don't weep
For we are bonded together
Like birds of a common feather
And just like salt and pepper
We will always go together
True friends and comrades too
When the snow lays deep, there will always be just me and you.

Our passion does often wane when the snow is deep;
I try for passion together, you choose to sleep
Old age has caused the snow outside to fall
When snow fell years ago, you and me would be having a ball
I fear for our loving togetherness in this modern world
Our feelings often compromised and often twirled.

We were once joined together as though we were one
Waking hand in hand, oh having so much fun in the sun
But now that snowfall forces each of us inside
And now your feelings you so do hide
Did I upset you when I woke you from your sound sleep?
I am so so sorry… your inattentiveness doth cause me to

weep.

My love, you and I will find our place one day again—
Perhaps we will be joined together up there in heaven
Where there exists love and joy and no snow falls
You and me joined at the hip once again… we will have such a ball!

Love Is Lost

We two were lovers once
Now we are only friends
Where did all the glamour go?
Why did it have to end?

When our youth had lost its glow
And so harsh the sunlight's ray
In ripples along life's stream
Why did our love lose its way?

His body still abides
And he is always kind
But to some far-off place
Has gone my lover's mind.

In friendship there is peace
So true he stays my friend
Dreaming of my lover's touch
This seems to be the end.

Yes, we were lovers once
And now we are but friends—
So sad that such a beautiful thing
Should never have to end.

The Tides of Life

Please lay your body next to mine
And just let me please hold your hand
I know our heated passion has gone –
Oh, my dear beloved one, this I understand.

True love is of a spirit born
And the years of life will span
So lay your body close to mine
While I hold onto your unsteady hand.

Many tides of life do leave us so frail
From life's shore the tides wash the sand
But while I feel you so close, my love
This makes me feel so very grand.

You will always be my lovely rose
That always blooms in my heart
So while I can still hold your hand
You and me, together, we will never part.

Just to know that you are close
Keeps me so happy and so content –
For you will always be my true love
That, to me, my good Lord has sent.

Such Is Life

Quiet Waters

I sit beside quiet calming waters
At peace with all the world around
Begone oh my fear with all its problems
Each so readily do bring me down.

Hark, I hear the voice of Jesus saying
"Come poor weary one… do not fall apart!"
For He too was often so very weary
And so alone and sad of heart.

So I gaze into those silver waters
That reflect nought of earthly care
But just goes on so gently flowing
Out to that huge ocean waiting out there.

Please my heart be still and in order
Try to stay calm in a perfect storm;
Be like sunbeams falling onto water
Oh so shimmering… always warm.

Then to my heart the waters do speak
To a peace beyond earth… amen!
Beyond this world of foul pollution

Far from the foolishness of men.

So often I go to sit beside the silver waters
When life's burdens become hard to bear
You who once walked on those silver waters
You come too and hold my hand.

I feel Your presence by those waters
When my need of You becomes so great
Then I feel in my heart there is order
As I sit, think, and mediate.

So speak to me oh silver waters:
Tell me of the One now here by my side
Tell me about His peace and calm
And of His teachings I will abide.

My Days

To live my days beneath your care
To know that you will always be there
To give me courage to banish my fear
Of ugly things that hover so near.

To give my heart your own sweet peace
When all around wars seem to never cease
To give out love to those in need—
These are the things for which I plead.

These earthly days…they fly so fast
And not forever they will last
So let them be as music so sweet
Floating around one's dancing feet.

If in the shadow of thy love
I can be as a gentle dove
And ever be in sweet accord
Then I can live to please my Lord.

Dark Planet

As I journey on this modern earth
That holds little hallowed light
This is my ever-fervent prayer:
Please Jesus… help me through each night!

There are dark shadows so very grim
Oft hover in my sight
When these draw near, I call to thee:
Please Jesus… help me through the night!

There are things I dare not to face
And things so very hard to fight
So I must seek a higher strength
Please Jesus…help me through the night!

'Till there breaks a brand-new dawn'
And dark shadows have fled with night
'Till I am safely in my home once more'
Please Jesus… help me through the night!

Suffer the Little Children

Mum and Dad had an argument last night
Seems all they do is accuse and fight
I seldom sleep… I am so afraid
What happens if they separate?
What of me and of little Sue?
Where would we go?
What will we do?

The hurt we feel goes very deep;
I hear Sue always crying to sleep
My dad yells and my mum screams;
These angry voices haunt my dreams
Remember us… your little kids!
Before you put your marriage on the skids!

Why should all our lives be pulled apart
Because of argument that should never start?
Please stop and think of Sue and me
Before you start to disagree
Please give us little ones a go
So we can happily grow.

My teacher suspects I am a fool
Because I am slow of learning in school;
She does not know about the fear and dread

That spins around inside my head
The fear of loss and of change
The dread of starting a new life… so strange.

My God of love you command from above
Please help my parents show more love
They wanted us here… now they don't seem to care!
Just selfishness… they are so aware
A happy marriage they cannot boast
When little kids are hurt the most!

The Gambler

It's just a game, a harmless game
They say, and this is their cry
"I can always give it up!"
But most do not until they die.

It is an awful game, a deadly game
That can tear your life to shreds
Chasing elusive rainbows
But getting stuck in mud instead.

Crowns and empires have been lost
When playing these addictive games
And often a once happy life
Will never be the same again.

It is like a poison in your blood
Creeps in and pulls you down
Within the game that seeks to tame
A raging tempest can be found.

It calls to you like some evil God
A force you cannot control;
It will rob you of your dignity
By permeating into your soul.

Like a phantom beckoning you to go on
Showing you a dreaming in the sky
Dame fortune keeps laughing up her sleeve
At those who chance and try.

She flaunts a mirage at their face
That keeps them keeping on
And when the last chance has past
All love and hope are then gone.

The Alcoholic

So lonely in his muddled world
Hemmed in by despair
No ray of hope, no beam of joy
Will never enter there
Whose hands will reach into the depths
To help him face the sun?
Who will lament his passing on
When his tortured journey is done?

He worries not about worldly affairs
Nor who will walk the moon
He will often burst with hungry thirst;
For drink, more drink, and soon
His chief delight be wine by sight
And the taste of sparkling ale
It matters not how it be got;
The getting must not fail.

He will rob his children and his wife
Of their essential bread and butter;
The raging thirst, it must come first
His life heading for the gutter
He knows full well the taste of hell
Is so bitter on his tongue
He tries to fight to reach the light

But his hungry thirst has come.

Now who will tear his bondage away
And save his helpless mind?
So that he can become a man again
And mix with humankind
His nights are filled with the devil's pull;
He sees ghastly things, and spiders that crawl;
His mind so groggy, so very full –
They cover all his wall.

Fevered dreams bring forth horrid screams
Night terrors fill up his head
Pink elephants and three headed frogs
keep dancing on his bed
He dares not sleep but only drink
The dark night hours away
The things that creep won't let him sleep;
They all want him to come and play.

Now who will extend their helping hand
And so drive out the demon's spell?
That evil drink that has a kink
Can drive a drinker to hell
Who will heed the warning note
The message in this poem?
Do not drink—just stop and think!
Too many will ruin your home!

Too many walk that shadowed road
Self-respect is not their kin;

For friend fear walks there with despair
So sunshine just can't get in
And we who sleep so comfy and deep
Know nothing of the drinker's lair.
What can we know about where they go?

Because we have never been there.

Divorce

Drifting along a lonely road, you are not quite sure;
Feeling alienated from all that is safe and secure
Divorce is a lonely thing
The ties, now unbound, will still tug at your heart
It takes more than a thought to make a fresh start
Divorce is a lonely thing.

You yearn for a change, but it may be so strange;
You are like a lost boundary rider out on the range
Divorce is a lonely thing
Your life will be reset in a pattern anew
There will be times when you rue what you can't undo
Divorce is a lonely thing.

We often act in haste, so much anger to waste;
Some things forbidden, and often unchaste
Divorce is a lonely thing
We long for freedom from what does so bind
Seeking a new happiness, only to find
Divorce is a lonely thing.

You've scuttled your ship in which you sailed for so long
You feel so sick but maybe you are strong?
Divorce is a lonely thing
What kind of life will future years bring?

It could be remorse and sad songs to sing
Divorce is a lonely thing.

Maybe the Devil you know is a far better bet:
Turn around, look inside so you won't regret
Divorce is a lonely thing.

Try for one more time, open your feelings and shine
Hold out your olive branch, give it one more chance
because, Divorce is a lonely thing.

Who Inside?

Standing on a cliff so steep and wide
No one was there to hasten to his side
Crying and screaming like a little kid
One step forward, he almost slid.

Memories of her filled his eyes with tears
For they had been married for many many years;
Their life had been such a happy one
With her and their brand-new son
Until the day all three when out to dine
And there he drank far too much wine.

He lamented on that cliff, "*Why did I drive?*"
"*If I'd stopped my loved ones would still be alive.*"

"*So where they have gone I am going too,*"
"*And there is absolutely nothing anyone can do.*"

He yelled to himself, "*I just can't think!*"
As he stood there looking over the brink
That rocky surface beckoning to him below
Where all the swirling sea waters do flow.

"*I'm so sorry for this, dear Mum and Dad,*"
"*I know I'm the only child you had,*"

"To bring an end to it would not be bad…"
"But why do I feel like a bloody cad?"

He turned away from those swirling waters below
And towards safety he did go
He sat for a while and then let it all out
Then there was no more angst, no more shout.

We all possess two voices inside:
One is out there, the other one will hide
And plot destruction unless we recognise
That life can be full of enterprise.

We make mistakes… all of us do
But to suicide will not help us through
Remember life is about faith and trust
So don't listen to that negative voice inside us.

If you feel you have reached the end
Turn around three times and count to ten
Look towards Heaven and God will then send
Energy for you to start again!

Ageing

Nothing Lasts Forever

Youth, oh sweet youth
You have not learned wisdom
Nor looked for the truth
You fear not old age
For it seems so far away
But life is so short;
Old age will catch up with you one day.

Oft wasted are those years
That should be held so dear
And wisdom comes only
When old age draws near
You romp around in green meadows
With so much youth in your hands
Till the green grass around you withers
Where your feet now stand.

For old man time gives you no favours
Nor will he stand still
Each life has a purpose
That we should fulfil.

Youth is such a bright bubble

That floats around for a while
Then slowly descents with
Each earthly mile.

Soon comes the time when
We turn around
And discover with dismay
Our feet on the ground.

Gone are the frontiers
Of youth's excellent day
And they never come back—
Yearn though you may
When music has ceased
And so has the fun
Then you must admit
That old age has come.

Old Oak Tree

For you, my sweet child… life's journey has just begun
So play your games, my dear little one
Life can be rewarding… it can be fun
When you have only just turned one.

I tell you I feel just like an old oak tree
Because I have just turned seventy-three
I click my heels but can dance no more;
My legs ache… my feet are often so sore
No longer can I paint the town red
So I spend most of my time in bed.

When I can't walk… then I will hop around
Just like those little sparrows on the ground
But you can bet your life I won't be beat
Occasionally I can remove those shackles from my feet
And I tell you if Father time hangs around my door
Then he is going to cop it… that is for sure!

It is so strange to think that once I was one
And mischief to me was so much fun
When my life had just begun
Just like you are now, sweet little one.

So play your happy games, my little grandchild

Before life's road turns rough and wild;
Enjoy your time of just being one
Before those trials through your life do come.

Pity

We who are the old and sit and wait to die
Each with our guardian angel standing by
To separate each of us from our mould of clay
And then gently to guide our souls away.

Don't pity us if we choose to stay
There in one place, oft day by day
Our needs are just some loving care:
A nice soft bed, a comfy chair.

We've turned our eyes and ears away from worldly things
Those awful places where corruption clings;
We sense our final gate is opening wide
To allow our tired souls inside.

Don't pity us because we are slow
And cannot match the pace you go
We're weary of life's busy grind;
It is peaceful to be left behind.

Don't pity us because we lie
With vacant mouths and open eyes
Our astral body seeks to walk abroad—
Now straining at our silver chord.

We're waiting for the Lord's command
And the touch of his Angel's hand
Just pity what we do endure
Before the everlasting cure.

Don't pity us because we go
From out of your world you love and know
Our worn-out bodies watch and wait
For that open door… that golden gate.

Don't pity us; we will soon be free
Of all earth's shackles and accompanying misery
We the old who will soon cease to roam
Now our angel waits to guide us home.

Church on the Hill

She said, "*Ron, I must go to the church to pray,*"
"*For the sins of you; for the sins of me,*"
"*For the sins of the world today.*"
She went inside where candles gleam
And she knelt at the altar there
She bowed her humble head and then many prayers she said
For a cruel hard world that no longer cared.

He waited long at the old church door
For he feared to go within;
His heart was rife with careless strife
And the weight of his worldly sin
But the darkness came as she tarried long
And the man he so wearily grew
Yet few would pray for a world today
And her need was so great… he knew.

He then walked the aisle past the virgin's smile
And then knelt by his loved one's side.
"*Little kid, we must go because the north wind doth blow, and the dark clouds gather and collide.*"
Now Satan decided he didn't like this pair;
He felt they may undo his chaotic plan
So from the bell tower he did scornfully stare
And with his evil beady eyes he did scan.

Satan sneered as they drew so near
Moving out through the old church door
They who dared to pray for the world today
The Devil would see that they prayed no more
He roused the wind to a frenzied spin
Till it tore at the woman's shawl
And it tried to fling this bond of love thing
Up hard against the old church wall.

Then the woman cried as the wind grew wild;
She called for deliverance from the storm
Soon the fury went as though it were spent
And so the night grew still and warm
Now the trembling man took the woman's hand
These two who had dared to pray
And then they walked away from that church door
Where they had entered to pray for the world that day.

Death

Dora's beloved grandson, Laurie, was a boxer. Laurie followed in her husband Ronald's footsteps.

– *Lord Christopher*

The Boxer

Ricky Regan was his fighting name;
Many fights he had won
So very famous in the boxing ring
As the one who always made the run
There are many who would remember him
In all those days gone by
He was a tough young street fighter
Who had no fear for any guy.

But when that grim leukaemia
Appeared upon his youthful scene
Young Ricky then knew that fighting
For *fighting for his life* would mean
This fight was his hardest
That any young lad could endure
He gave it all his punches—
Of winning this fight… he was so sure.

That very brave young Ricky Regan
He fought and fought 'till the last
This fighter had so much to live for;
He had many plans he had made –
Just knock out this tough opponent
Then he would make the grade.

But like an insidious reptile
It wound its slimy length
So took his sight and hearing
And then slowly took his strength
No boxer ever battled
Such a horrid deadly foe
Although he fought on bravely
It just would not let him go.

And now young Ricky Regan
Has gone down for the count
Leukaemia was the eventual winner
His white blood cells they did mount
Yet even then he struggled and struggled
Before the count of ten
He refused to go down defeated;
He sought to rise and rise again
But death was fast approaching –
He took his final stand
And now a brave street fighter
Has gone missing from our land.

Farewell young Ricky Regan

Such fighters just like you
Make us bow in awe of such valour.

You showed us all your derring-do!

The following two poems were penned shortly after Dora's husband Ronald passed away from prostate cancer.

Lord Christopher

Suddenly Alone

There are so many widows… so it seems
Bereft of all their earthly dreams
No more a husbands' hand to hold
No more his loving arms will enfold.

Now loneliness has come to live and dwell
So much pain… this must be hell!
I constantly call to him but no response is there
For he has left our loving family home… and my care.

Dim now that which was so much aglow
Oh God… why did my true love have to go?
Farewell my Prince, the love of my heart
You suffered so long… then we had to part.

I was too late to say to you *"good-bye"*
You floated so swiftly through that sky.

I still say *"we"* as though you are still here –

Oh! how I wish you were still so very near.

For those of us who have had such true love known
Sad now is our path… we have no choice but to walk alone
No one could love me so much as my Prince did
His pet name for me was "*little kid*".

Oh, how I long to hear that pet name again
To stop me from going, at times, insane
You know I will soldier on (oh yes, my love)
Until we are together again… like hand to glove
This is the way that sadly we all must go
Oh, my dearly beloved, I miss you so!

Pilgrim's Journey

My true love has arrived in the Garden of God
And I tell you never a rose was so fair
I think he would wish me not to sadly mourn
For he is now free from earth's trouble and care.

He is tended now by soft Angel hands
There is something he would like you to know –
He will be standing and waiting to welcome you there
When also to the garden you will go.

God's ways we may not always understand
And oft so bitter we turn from His love
But all will be righted when we go
To that beautiful garden to join with Ron high above.

God Is Calling

Highway to Heaven

I had a vision that I was running and dancing along
By the banks of several beautiful streams
My body was as light as the sweetly scented air
Being bathed in the sun's beautiful beams
My mind was as free as all those birds in the trees
Away from all of life's bustles and cares
The sky above seemed to be of
A shade of such heavenly blue
I sang an engaging song as I danced along
And the beautiful streams sang along with me too.

Such beauty I saw as never before;
I have never seen this on our earthly plane
This was a place of much beauty and space
Away from all living sorrow and pain.

It soon became clear I was drifting quite near
A highway through that heavenly blue
Then alas that old earth summoned me back
And my heavenly vision faded from view.

Tomorrow

We all search for tomorrow
looking for its joy... not it's sorrow
Then when we find it
It is but our day... this day
Strength that we may borrow
From thoughts of tomorrow
Yet there could be problems
The same all the way
For time is unceasing
And life is but a leasing
When every tomorrow
Becomes but another today
So let each tomorrow
Take care of its sorrow
And live for the blessings
That came to you today.

New Life

Death is Life

During my last day… He did appear before me
He reached out and stilled my unsteady hand;
He then softly spoke, *"Please come with me and see
What I am doing for thee in your land."*
He led me out of my valley of sadness and despair;
My heart then ceased all of its pinning
Then I knew my Lord… our creator was with me there
He beckoned me to follow Him up Heaven's mountain;
There I discovered His healing breeze doth blow.

He whispered to me, *"Do not despair…
I am with you… can you see?"*
Heavens soft winds then did blow all of my sadness away
He then proudly announced, *"I have reserved a place for thee!"*
And then He whispered, *"You are much loved, little kid… Your
beloved Ronald waits for Yee."*

I now know there are no boundaries set around His love
It is so grand… far wider than the widest sea;
God's love reaches all around our material world
His love is providence for both you and me!